365 Quotes to Live Your Life By

Powerful, Inspiring, & Life-Changing Words of Wisdom to Brighten Up Your Days

By I. C. Robledo

365 Quotes to Live Your Life By: Powerful, Inspiring, & Life-Changing Words of Wisdom to Brighten Up Your Days

Disclaimer

Table of Contents

Introducing the *365 Quotes to Live Your Life By*

"The wisdom of the wise, and the experience of ages, may be preserved by quotation."

— Isaac D'Israeli —

The Purpose of this Book

This book is meant to function as a companion to *7 Thoughts to Live Your Life By: A Guide to the Happy, Peaceful, & Meaningful Life*. You may read *365 Quotes to Live Your Life By* before, after, or alongside it. A free excerpt of *7 Thoughts to Live Your Life By* is included at the end of this book for you to learn more about the project.

Here is a brief overview of the 7 Thoughts, so that you can see the key themes we will cover in this book:

1. **Focus on what you can control, *not* on what you cannot control**
2. **Focus on the positive, *not* the negative**
3. **Focus on what you can do, *not* on what you cannot do**
4. **Focus on what you have, *not* on what you do not have**
5. **Focus on the present, *not* on the past and future**
6. **Focus on what you need, *not* on what you want**
7. **Focus on what you can give, *not* on what you can take**

Having these Thoughts every day has changed my life for the better, and I believe that they can help you as well. They are so important that I decided it would be valuable to create a book of quotes that supports these Thoughts.

1

Many great people and leaders have stated wise words that support the *7 Thoughts*, and they are compiled here for you. If you are not interested in the *7 Thoughts to Live Your Life By*, then that is no problem – just read the quotes and enjoy them for what they are – inspiring and uplifting words of wisdom. Although, keep in mind that what makes this book of quotes unique is that it is based on a system of thinking that you can use to build a better life for yourself.

If you have never read a book of quotes before, I would like to emphasize that reading the right quote at the right time in your life can leave an immense impression upon you. The trick is to find just the right words that you need to hear at just the right time, for you to find the courage to make the changes that you know will steer you on the right path. The words themselves do not change the world – but your sensing that the words are true, truer than anything you've ever seen or known or touched, this is what makes them jump off the page and give you the will to make those words come to life.

These quotes of wisdom are so powerful that I aim to remember all the words in them and to recall who said them. Of course, these are words I aim to apply in my life every day. I share them in conversations and use them to uplift and inspire when I sense that someone needs to hear them. Now I will share them with you. Allow these words to guide you and help you to become the better person that you always knew you could be.

How the Quotes were Selected, Compiled, and Organized

As mentioned, the quotes herein were specifically selected to support the *7 Thoughts to Live Your Life By*. Every quote will support one of those Thoughts in some way. In some cases, this book may appear to be repetitious as there are 365 quotes that support just 7 Thoughts, but I believe that we should spend more time focusing on the most critical thoughts and ideas, rather than allowing ourselves to become distracted in every possible direction. Ultimately, you will absorb the key Thoughts through a multitude of quotes, to truly understand them on a level that is deeper than words and that drives you to take positive daily actions.

Keep in mind that we have thousands of thoughts per day. You should guide your mind to have more of the thoughts that are truly worth having, rather than allowing it to move in directions that are unproductive and self-defeating.

These are quotes that I found moving and helpful and that I think we could all benefit from incorporating into our lives. I searched through thousands of quotes by authors, leaders, scientists, artists, and other important people to compile this special list. An important criterion for me was that the quote should focus on something positive we can do, rather than simply pointing out negative aspects of our human nature. This book is meant to lift us up and brighten our days, not to drag us down and darken them.

My aim was to select quotes from a broad range of time periods, cultures, regions, age ranges, and from men and women, but not all groups are well accounted for in the historical records, thus we cannot expect a perfect representation of groups in this selection of quotes. Thank you for your understanding.

Note that all attempts have been made to maintain the accuracy of the quotes and giving credit to the original source. In many instances where words such as "man," "men," or "mankind" were used, they can be assumed to apply to both men and women or to humankind. Likewise, I believe that the quotes which mention women can also apply to men. I have not altered any of the quotes in any way and in a few cases, they may also contain slang or unconventional grammar.

Ultimately, I believe that a repetition of the quotes will have the greatest positive impact on your life. You can read a phrase once and it may leave no impact. But coming back to it again and again may leave a deeper impression upon you and help you to apply it and actualize it in your life.

Lastly, I would like you to note that as I have aimed to make this book beneficial to all groups, no quotes with curse words or offensive language have been used. This book is intended to help everyone meet their life goals and fulfill their dreams in a way that helps us to elevate the consciousness and spirit of all of humanity.

Focus on What You Can Control, *Not* on What You Cannot Control

---

"You have power over your mind – not outside events. Realize this, and you will find strength." — Marcus Aurelius, *Meditations*

"Our life is shaped by our mind; we become what we think. Joy follows a pure thought like a shadow that never leaves." — Gautama Buddha

---

"Carefully watch your thoughts, for they become your words. Manage and watch your words, for they will become your actions. Consider and judge your actions, for they have become your habits. Acknowledge and watch your habits, for they shall become your values. Understand and embrace your values, for they become your destiny." — Mahatma Gandhi

---

"No matter what your choices are, you truly have no control about what people think of you."— Neve Campbell

---

"There is only one way to happiness and that is to cease worrying about things which are beyond the power of our will." — Epictetus, *The Philosophy of Epictetus*

"The only thing you sometimes have control over is perspective. You don't have control over your situation. But you have a choice about how you view it." — Chris Pine

"Some of our struggles involve making decisions, while others are a result of the decisions we have made. Some of our struggles result from choices others make that affect our lives. We cannot always control everything that happens to us in this life, but we can control how we respond. Many struggles come as problems and pressures that sometimes cause pain. Others come as temptations, trials, and tribulations." — L. Lionel Kendrick

"At the end of the day, you are in control of your own happiness. Life is going to happen whether you overthink it, overstress it or not. Just experience life and be happy along the way. You can't control everything in your life, but you can control your happiness."— Holly Holm

"I can control my destiny, but not my fate. Destiny means there are opportunities to turn right or left, but fate is a one-way street. I believe we all have the choice as to whether we fulfill our destiny, but our fate is sealed." — Paulo Coelho

"There is a lot that happens around the world we cannot control. We cannot stop earthquakes, we cannot prevent droughts, and we cannot prevent all conflict, but when we know where the hungry, the homeless and the sick exist, then we can help." — Jan Schakowsky

"I can be changed by what happens to me. But I refuse to be reduced by it." — Maya Angelou, *Letter to My Daughter*

"Why worry? If you have done the very best you can. Worrying won't make it any better. If you want to be successful, respect one rule: Never let failure take control of you." — Leonardo DiCaprio

"Inspiration is one thing and you can't control it, but hard work is what keeps the ship moving. Good luck means, work hard. Keep up the good work." — Kevin Eubanks

"After one has been in prison, it is the small things that one appreciates: being able to take a walk whenever one wants, going into a shop and buying a newspaper, speaking or choosing to remain silent. The simple act of being able to control one's person." — Nelson Mandela

"Control what you can control. Don't lose sleep worrying about things that you don't have control over because, at the end of the day, you still won't have any control over them." — Cam Newton

"Regardless of how you feel inside, always try to look like a winner. Even if you are behind, a sustained look of control and confidence can give you a mental edge that results in victory." — Arthur Ashe

"I'm not the perfect person. I'm not the most happy person. I get angry, and I get mad sometimes, but I try my best to control my thoughts. Because that flows throughout your body." — Karrueche Tran

"I can only control myself, my actions, my work ethic, and my attitude." — Ali Krieger

"The highest possible stage in moral culture is when we recognize that we ought to control our thoughts." — Charles Darwin, *The Descent of Man*

"Negative emotions will challenge your grit every step of the way. While it's impossible not to feel your emotions, it's completely under your power to manage them effectively and to keep yourself in a position of control. When you let your emotions overtake your ability to think clearly, it's easy to lose your resolve." — Travis Bradberry

"I don't get upset over things I can control, because if I can control them there's no sense in getting upset. And I don't get upset over things I can't control, because if I can't control them there's no sense in getting upset." — Mickey Rivers

"It's easy to fall into victim mode and feel like the world is against you. The truth is, people aren't against you: they're just for themselves. The only thing within your control is how you react and respond to the chaotic dance of life." — Kerli

"To enjoy freedom we have to control ourselves." — Virginia Woolf

"Bottom line, I removed myself from the victim mentality and took control of my life. I'm not just going to take responsibility for the success in my life – I'm going to take responsibility for the failures in my life. When you're willing to accept that you're the problem, you immediately become the solution." — Eric D. Thomas

"One of the hard lessons to learn in life is that there are some things you can control and some things you can't. If you want a short recipe for being frustrated and miserable, this is it: focus on things you can't control." — John Bytheway

"One of the things I realized is that if you do not take control over your time and your life, other people will gobble it up. If you don't prioritize yourself, you constantly start falling lower and lower on your list, your kids fall lower and lower on your list." — Michelle Obama

"The best years of your life are the ones in which you decide your problems are your own. You do not blame them on your mother, the ecology, or the president. You realize that you control your own destiny." — Albert Ellis

"The secret of success is learning how to use pain and pleasure instead of having pain and pleasure use you. If you do that, you're in control of your life. If you don't, life controls you." — Tony Robbins

"Talent without effort is wasted talent. And while effort is the one thing you can control in your life, applying that effort intelligently is next on the list." — Mark Cuban

"If you drill down on any success story, you always discover that luck was a huge part of it. You can't control luck, but you can move from a game with bad odds to one with better odds. You can make it easier for luck to find you. The most useful thing you can do is stay in the game." — Scott Adams

"The sign of an intelligent people is their ability to control their emotions by the application of reason." — Marya Mannes, *More in Anger*

"There is a core independence and dignity you get when you control your own time." — Travis Kalanick

"Women need to be empowered to shape their own livelihoods and become CEOs of their own lives. They must be allowed to take control of important life decisions that are so often decided by others." — Philomena Kwao

"Mastering others is strength. Mastering yourself is true power." — Lao Tzu, *Tao Te Ching*

"Everything can be taken from a man but one thing: the last of human freedoms – to choose one's attitude in any given set of circumstances, to choose one's own way." — Viktor E. Frankl, *Man's Search For Meaning*

"There can be only one permanent revolution — a moral one; the regeneration of the inner man. How is this revolution to take place? Nobody knows how it will take place in humanity, but every man feels it clearly in himself. And yet in our world everybody thinks of changing humanity, and nobody thinks of changing himself." — Leo Tolstoy, *Pamphlets*

"To enjoy good health, to bring true happiness to one's family, to bring peace to all, one must first discipline and control one's own mind. If a man can control his mind he can find the way to Enlightenment, and all wisdom and virtue will naturally come to him." — Gautama Buddha

"The greatest discovery of my generation is that people can alter their lives simply by altering their attitude of mind." — William James

"Each of us makes our own weather, determines the color of the skies in the emotional universe which we inhabit." — Fulton J. Sheen

"Everything you do, every thought you have, every word you say creates a memory that you will hold in your body. It's imprinted on you and affects you in subtle ways – ways you are not always aware of. With that in mind, be very conscious and selective." — Phylicia Rashad

"Repetition of the same thought or physical action develops into a habit which, repeated frequently enough, becomes an automatic reflex." — Norman Vincent Peale, *Enthusiasm Makes the Difference*

"I believe the ability to think is blessed. If you can think about a situation, you can deal with it. The big struggle is to keep your head clear enough to think." — Richard Pryor

"I understand more and more how true Daddy's words were when he said: 'All children must look after their own upbringing.' Parents can only give good advice or put them on the right paths, but the final forming of a person's character lies in their own hands." — Anne Frank, *The Diary of a Young Girl*

"It all begins and ends in your mind. What you give power to has power over you." — Leon Brown

"Attitude is a choice. Happiness is a choice. Optimism is a choice. Kindness is a choice. Giving is a choice. Respect is a choice. Whatever choice you make makes you. Choose wisely." — Roy T. Bennett, *The Light in the Heart*

"When the whole world is silent, even one voice becomes powerful."

— Malala Yousafzai

"You are the master of your destiny. You can influence, direct and control your own environment. You can make your life what you want it to be." — Napoleon Hill

"Success is hastened or delayed by one's habits. It is not your passing inspirations or brilliant ideas so much as your everyday mental habits that control your life." — Paramahansa Yogananda, *The Law of Success*

"Seek always for the answer within. Be not influenced by those around you, by their thoughts or their words." — Eileen Caddy, *God Spoke to Me*

"If you're always in a hurry, always trying to get ahead of the other guy, or someone else's performance is what motivates you, then that person is in control of you." — Wayne Dyer

"Never allow anyone to rain on your parade and thus cast a pall of gloom and defeat on the entire day. Remember that no talent, no self-denial, no brains, no character, are required to set up in the fault-finding business. Nothing external can have any power over you unless you permit it. Your time is too precious to be sacrificed in wasted days combating the menial forces of hate, jealously, and envy. Guard your fragile life carefully. Only God can shape a flower, but any foolish child can pull it to pieces." — Og Mandino, *A Better Way to Live*

Before You Continue . . .

As a thank you for reading, I want you to have this free guide:

Step Up Your Learning: Free Tools to Learn Almost Anything

Although learning tools may appear to be a completely different topic than the one this book covers, I believe strongly that we should *always* be learning something so that we can meet our full potential as human beings. Remember that you are always able to learn about any topic that is important to you. I recommend that you focus on areas you are curious about, or that can help you to get one step closer to your dream job or dream life.

This guide stems from my own experiences of using a variety of learning sites and resources. In it, you will discover the best places to go for learning at no cost. Also, I'll explain which resources are best for you, depending on your learning goals.

You can download this free guide as a PDF by typing this website into your browser: http://mentalmax.net/EN

Now, let's get back on topic.

Focus on the Positive, *Not* the Negative

"Life is an opportunity, benefit from it. Life is a beauty, admire it. Life is a dream, realize it. Life is a challenge, meet it. Life is a duty, complete it. Life is a game, play it. Life is a promise, fulfill it. Life is sorrow, overcome it. Life is a song, sing it. Life is a struggle, accept it. Life is a tragedy, confront it. Life is an adventure, dare it. Life is luck, make it. Life is life, fight for it!" — Mother Teresa

"It is during our darkest moments that we must focus to see the light." — Aristotle Onassis

"Don't forget to tell yourself positive things daily! You must love yourself internally to glow externally." — Hannah Bronfman

"Let us read and let us dance; these two amusements will never do any harm to the world." — Voltaire, *The Works of Voltaire*

"Surround yourself with only people who are going to lift you higher." — Oprah Winfrey

"If you realized how powerful your thoughts are, you would never think a negative thought." — Peace Pilgrim, *Peace Pilgrim*

"Adventure begins with you, personally. It is in the way you look at things. It is the mental stance you take as you face your day. It is finding magic in things. It is talking with people and discovering their inner goodness. It is the thrill of feeling a part of the life around you. The attitude of adventure will open things up for you. The world will become alive with new zest and meaning. You'll become more aware of the beauty everywhere. Nothing will seem unimportant. Everything will be revealed as having pattern and purpose." — Wilferd Peterson

"The happiness of your life depends upon the quality of your thoughts: therefore, guard accordingly, and take care that you entertain no notions unsuitable to virtue and reasonable nature." — Marcus Aurelius, *The Emperor Marcus Antoninus*

"Darkness cannot drive out darkness; only light can do that. Hate cannot drive out hate; only love can do that." — Martin Luther King, Jr., *A Gift of Love*

"What you do not want done to yourself, do not do to others." — Confucius, *The Analects*

"A pessimist is one who makes difficulties of his or her opportunities; an optimist is one who makes opportunities of his or her difficulties." — Harry S. Truman

"Almost all our suffering is the product of our thoughts. We spend nearly every moment of our lives lost in thought, and hostage to the character of those thoughts. You can break this spell, but it takes training just like it takes training to defend yourself against a physical assault." — Sam Harris

"Stay positive and happy. Work hard and don't give up hope. Be open to criticism and keep learning. Surround yourself with happy, warm and genuine people." — Tina Desai

"Once you replace negative thoughts with positive ones, you'll start having positive results." — Willie Nelson, *The Tao of Willie*

"Work hard for what you want because it won't come to you without a fight. You have to be strong and courageous and know that you can do anything you put your mind to. If somebody puts you down or criticizes you, just keep on believing in yourself and turn it into something positive." — Leah LaBelle

"Find a place inside where there's joy, and the joy will burn out the pain." — Joseph Campbell

"I think that life is difficult. People have challenges. Family members get sick, people get older, you don't always get the job or the promotion that you want. You have conflicts in your life. And really, life is about your resilience and your ability to go through your life and all of the ups and downs with a positive attitude." — Jennifer Hyman

"ALWAYS remember, we all have our own opinions and beliefs. We have different ways in dealing with life's troubles and joys. To survive our differences without hurting each other is what GOODNESS is all about." — Dodinsky

"Did I offer peace today? Did I bring a smile to someone's face? Did I say words of healing? Did I let go of my anger and resentment? Did I forgive? Did I love? These are the real questions. I must trust that the little bit of love that I sow now will bear many fruits, here in this world and the life to come." — Henri Nouwen

"If you have a positive attitude and constantly strive to give your best effort, eventually you will overcome your immediate problems and find you are ready for greater challenges." — Pat Riley

"I realized that if my thoughts immediately affect my body, I should be careful about what I think. Now if I get angry, I ask myself why I feel that way. If I can find the source of my anger, I can turn that negative energy into something positive." — Yoko Ono

"Positive thinking will let you do everything better than negative thinking will." — Zig Ziglar

"In every day, there are 1,440 minutes. That means we have 1,440 daily opportunities to make a positive impact." — Les Brown

"Be not afraid of life. Believe that life is worth living and your belief will help create the fact." — William James, *The Will to Believe and Other Essays in Popular Philosophy*

"Stop saying these negative things about yourself. Look in the mirror and find something about yourself that's positive and celebrate that!" — Tyra Banks

"If someone says something hurtful to you or makes you feel down on yourself, then you just gotta stay positive and keep moving forward because they might not know much about you, or they may not understand the situation." — Jazz Jennings

"It takes but one positive thought when given a chance to survive and thrive to overpower an entire army of negative thoughts." — Robert H. Schuller

"I truly believe the intention of creating positive change is so important to the collective consciousness. When you have a group of people that have the intention and the capacity, talent, and intelligence to actualize those intentions, then you have something really powerful." — Jimmy Chin

"Winners make a habit of manufacturing their own positive expectations in advance of the event." — Brian Tracy

"Being positive is like going up a mountain. Being negative is like sliding down a hill. A lot of times, people want to take the easy way out, because it's basically what they've understood throughout their lives." — Chuck D

"Keep away from people who try to belittle your ambitions. Small people always do that, but the really great make you feel that you, too, can become great." — Mark Twain, *Mark Twain at Your Fingertips*

"To be healthy, wealthy, happy and successful in any and all areas of your life you need to be aware that you need to think healthy, wealthy, and happy and successful thoughts twenty-four hours a day and cancel all negative, destructive, fearful and unhappy thoughts. These two types of thoughts cannot coexist if you want to share in the abundance that surrounds us all." — Sydney Madwed

"The first question to be answered by any individual or any social group, facing a hazardous situation, is whether the crisis is to be met as a challenge to strength or as an occasion for despair." — Harry Emerson Fosdick, *The Challenge of the Present Crisis*

"Happiness is when what you think, what you say, and what you do are in harmony." — Mahatma Gandhi

"I believe that every single event in life happens in an opportunity to choose love over fear." — Oprah Winfrey

"We think sometimes that poverty is only being hungry, naked and homeless. The poverty of being unwanted, unloved and uncared for is the greatest poverty. We must start in our own homes to remedy this kind of poverty." — Mother Teresa

"The beginning of love is to let those we love be perfectly themselves, and not to twist them to fit our own image. Otherwise we love only the reflection of ourselves we find in them." — Thomas Merton, *No Man is an Island*

"Beginning today, treat everyone you meet as if they were going to be dead by midnight. Extend to them all the care, kindness and understanding you can muster, and do it with no thought of any reward. Your life will never be the same again." — Og Mandino

"The greatness of a man is not in how much wealth he acquires, but in his integrity and his ability to affect those around him positively." — Bob Marley

"Please believe that one single positive dream is more important than a thousand negative realities." — Adeline Yen Mah, *Chinese Cinderella*

"When pain brings you down, don't be silly, don't close your eyes and cry, you just might be in the best position to see the sun shine." — Alanis Morissette

"We cannot selectively numb emotions, when we numb the painful emotions, we also numb the positive emotions." — Brené Brown, *The Gifts of Imperfection*

"There is a magnificent, beautiful, wonderful painting in front of you! It is intricate, detailed, a painstaking labor of devotion and love! The colors are like no other, they swim and leap, they trickle and embellish! And yet you choose to fixate your eyes on the small fly which has landed on it! Why do you do such a thing?" — C. JoyBell C.

"Of course there must be lots of Magic in the world," he said wisely one day, "but people don't know what it is like or how to make it. Perhaps the beginning is just to say nice things are going to happen until you make them happen. I am going to try and experiment." — Frances Hodgson Burnett, *The Secret Garden*

"Life is full of beauty. Notice it. Notice the bumblebee, the small child, and the smiling faces. Smell the rain, and feel the wind. Live your life to the fullest potential, and fight for your dreams." — Ashley Smith

"Don't be discouraged by a failure. It can be a positive experience. Failure is, in a sense, the highway to success, inasmuch as every discovery of what is false leads us to seek earnestly after what is true, and every fresh experience points out some form of error which we shall afterwards carefully avoid." — John Keats

"I am an optimist... I choose to be. There is a lot of darkness in our world, there is a lot of pain and you can choose to see that or you can choose to see the joy. If you try to respond positively to the world, you will spend your time better." — Tom Hiddleston

"The pursuit of happiness is a matter of choice... it is a positive attitude we choose to express. It is not a gift delivered to our door each morning, nor does it come through the window. And it is certain that our circumstances are not the things that make us joyful. If we wait for them to get just right, we will never laugh again." — Charles R. Swindoll, *Laugh Again Hope Again*

"Remember, you have been criticizing yourself for years and it hasn't worked. Try approving of yourself and see what happens." — Louise L. Hay, *You Can Heal Your Life*

"I hope you will have a wonderful year, that you'll dream dangerously and outrageously, that you'll make something that didn't exist before you made it, that you will be loved and that you will be liked, and that you will have people to love and to like in return. And, most importantly (because I think there should be more kindness and more wisdom in the world right now), that you will, when you need to be, be wise, and that you will always be kind." — Neil Gaiman

"If you can cultivate the right attitude, your enemies are your best spiritual teachers because their presence provides you with the opportunity to enhance and develop tolerance, patience and understanding." — Dalai Lama XIV, *The Good Heart*

"So, what if, instead of thinking about solving your whole life, you just think about adding additional good things. One at a time. Just let your pile of good things grow." — Rainbow Rowell, *Attachments*

Focus on What You Can Do, *Not* on What You Cannot Do

"If you can't fly then run, if you can't run then walk, if you can't walk then crawl, but whatever you do you have to keep moving forward." — Martin Luther King, Jr.

"Alone we can do so little; together we can do so much." — Helen Keller

---

"Do or do not. There is no try." — Yoda (George Lucas), *Star Wars: Episode V – The Empire Strikes Back*

"Always do your best. Your best is going to change from moment to moment; it will be different when you are healthy as opposed to sick. Under any circumstance, simply do your best, and you will avoid self-judgment, self-abuse and regret." — Don Miguel Ruiz, *The Four Agreements*

"If you don't like something, change it. If you can't change it, change your attitude."— Maya Angelou

---

"The most difficult thing is the decision to act, the rest is merely tenacity. The fears are paper tigers. You can do anything you decide to do. You can act to change and control your life; and the procedure, the process is its own reward." — Amelia Earhart

"We do not need magic to change the world, we carry all the power we need inside ourselves already: we have the power to imagine better." — J. K. Rowling, *Very Good Lives*

"We are what we repeatedly do. Excellence then, is not an act, but a habit." — Will Durant, *The Story of Philosophy*

"When something is important enough, you do it even if the odds are not in your favor." — Elon Musk

"It's not the absence of fear, it's overcoming it. Sometimes you've got to blast through and have faith." — Emma Watson

"You choose the life you live. If you don't like it, it's on you to change it because no one else is going to do it for you." — Kim Kiyosaki

"We always overestimate the change that will occur in the next two years and underestimate the change that will occur in the next ten. Don't let yourself be lulled into inaction." — Bill Gates, *Business @ the Speed of Thought*

"The journey of a thousand miles begins with one step." — Lao Tzu, *Tao Te Ching*

"Never give up. Today is hard, tomorrow will be worse, but the day after tomorrow will be sunshine." — Jack Ma

"Every human has four endowments – self-awareness, conscience, independent will and creative imagination. These give us the ultimate human freedom... The power to choose, to respond, to change." — Stephen Covey

"It's not what happens to you, but how you react to it that matters." — Epictetus

"When we are no longer able to change a situation – we are challenged to change ourselves." — Viktor E. Frankl, *Man's Search for Meaning*

"In dreams, anything can be anything, and everybody can do. We can fly, we can turn upside down, we can transform into anything." — Twyla Tharp

"In this life, you should read everything you can read. Taste everything you can taste. Meet everyone you can meet. Travel everywhere you can travel. Learn everything you can learn. Experience everything you can experience." — Mario Cuomo

"I urge you to try and create the world you want to live in. Minister to the world in a way that can change it. Minister radically in a real, active, practical, get your hands dirty way." — Chimimanda Ngozi Adiche

"Do all the good you can, by all the means you can, in all the ways you can, in all the places you can, at all the times you can, to all the people you can, as long as ever you can." — John Wesley, *Letters*

"When it is obvious that the goals cannot be reached, don't adjust the goals, adjust the action steps." — Confucius

"Just remember, you can do anything you set your mind to, but it takes action, perseverance, and facing your fears." — Gillian Anderson

"The way to change the world is through individual responsibility and taking local action in your own community." — Jeff Bridges

"To complain is always nonacceptance of what is. It invariably carries an unconscious negative charge. When you complain, you make yourself into a victim. When you speak out, you are in your power. So change the situation by taking action or by speaking out if necessary or possible; leave the situation or accept it. All else is madness."— Eckhart Tolle, *The Power of Now*

"Ask not what your country can do for you, ask what you can do for your country." — John F. Kennedy

"The question really is, are you improving the world? And you can do that in many models. You can do that in government, you can do that in a nonprofit, and you can do it in commercial enterprise." — Jeff Bezos

"If you can do something great in 60 seconds, you can do anything, really." — Joanne Froggatt

"Do the one thing you think you cannot do. Fail at it. Try again. Do better the second time. The only people who never tumble are those who never mount the high wire. This is your moment. Own it." — Oprah Winfrey

"Infuse your life with action. Don't wait for it to happen. Make it happen. Make your own future. Make your own hope. Make your own love. And whatever your beliefs, honor your creator, not by passively waiting for grace to come down from upon high, but by doing what you can to make grace happen... yourself, right now, right down here on Earth." — Bradley Whitford

"Twenty years from now you will be more disappointed by the things that you didn't do than by the ones you did do. So throw off the bowlines. Sail away from the safe harbor. Catch the trade winds in your sails. Explore. Dream. Discover." — H. Jackson Brown, Jr., *P.S. I Love You*

"God, grant me the serenity to accept the things I cannot change, the courage to change the things I can, and the wisdom to know the difference." — Reinhold Niebuhr

"Nothing in the world can take place of persistence. Talent will not; nothing is more common than unsuccessful individuals with talent. Genius will not; unrewarded genius is almost a proverb. Education will not; the world is full of educated derelicts. Persistence and determination alone are omnipotent." — Calvin Coolidge

"People who have attained things worth having in this world have worked while others idled, have persevered when others gave up in despair, have practiced early in life the valuable habits of self-denial, industry, and singleness of purpose. As a result, they enjoy later in life the success so often erroneously attributed to good luck." — Grenville Kleiser

"As long as you're actively pursuing your dream with a practical plan, you're still achieving, even if it feels as though you're going nowhere fast. It's been my experience that at the very moment I feel like giving up, I'm only one step from a breakthrough. Hang on long enough and circumstances will change, too. Trust in yourself, your dream and spirit." — Sarah Ban Breathnach

"Conditions are never just right. People who delay action until all factors are favorable do nothing." — William Feather

"We are responsible for what we are, and we wish ourselves to be, we have the power to make ourselves. If what we are now has been the result of our past actions, it certainly follows that whatever we wish to be in the future can be produced by our present actions; so we have to know how to act." — Swami Vivekananda, *Karma Yoga*

"It is in the whole process of meeting and solving problems that life has meaning. Problems are the cutting edge that distinguishes between success and failure. Problems call forth our courage and our wisdom; indeed, they create our courage and our wisdom. It is only because of problems that we grow mentally and spiritually. It is through the pain of confronting and resolving problems that we learn." — M. Scott Peck

"Unless you try to do something beyond what you have already mastered, you will never grow." — Ronald E. Osborn

"The ultimate measure of a man is not where he stands in moments of comfort and convenience, but where he stands at times of challenge and controversy." — Martin Luther King, Jr., *Strength to Love*

"If you have a dream, don't let anybody take it away and you always believe that the impossible is always possible." — Selena Quintanilla

"When you are laboring for others, let it be with the same zeal as if it were for yourself." — Confucius

"In the midst of chaos, there is also opportunity." — Sun Tzu, *The Art of War*

"Know how to listen and you will profit even from those who talk badly." — Plutarch

"One of life's fundamental truths states, 'Ask and you shall receive.' As kids we get used to asking for things, but somehow we lose this ability in adulthood. We come up with all sorts of excuses and reasons to avoid any possibility of criticism or rejection." — Jack Canfield

"Most of the important things in the world have been accomplished by people who have kept on trying when there seemed to be no hope at all." — Dale Carnegie, *How to Enjoy Your Life and Your Job*

"Change will not come if we wait for some other person or if we wait for some time. We are the ones we've been waiting for." — Barack Obama

"If there's a book you want to read, but it hasn't been written yet, then you must write it." — Toni Morrison

"We can change our lives. We can do, have, and be exactly what we wish." — Tony Robbins

"Be true to your own act, and congratulate yourself if you have done something strange and extravagant, and broken the monotony of a decorous age. It was a high counsel that I once heard given to a young person, 'Always do what you are afraid to do.'" — Ralph Waldo Emerson, *Heroism*

"You never really understand a person until you consider things from his point of view... Until you climb inside of his skin and walk around in it." — Atticus Finch (Harper Lee), *To Kill a Mockingbird*

"Treat people as if they were what they ought to be and you help them to become what they are capable of being." — Johann Wolfgang von Goethe

"I've learned that fear limits you and your vision. It serves as blinders to what may be just a few steps down the road for you. The journey is valuable, but believing in your talents, your abilities, and your self-worth can empower you to walk down an even brighter path. Transforming fear into freedom – how great is that?" — Soledad O'Brien

"Security is mostly a superstition. It does not exist in nature, nor do the children of men as a whole experience it. Avoiding danger is no safer in the long run than outright exposure. Life is either a daring adventure, or nothing." — Helen Keller, *The Open Door*

"Your time is limited, so don't waste it living someone else's life. Don't be trapped by dogma, which is living with the results of other people's thinking. Don't let the noise of other's opinions drown out your own inner voice. And most important, have the courage to follow your heart and intuition. They somehow already know what you truly want to become. Everything else is secondary." — Steve Jobs

"Never let life impede on your ability to manifest your dreams. Dig deeper into your dreams and deeper into yourself and believe that anything is possible, and make it happen." — Corin Nemec

"The place to improve the world is first in one's own heart and head and hands, and then work outward from there." — Robert M. Pirsig, *Zen and the Art of Motorcycle Maintenance*

"What we become depends on what we read after all of the professors have finished with us. The greatest university of all is a collection of books." — Thomas Carlyle

Focus on What You Have,
Not on What You Do Not Have

"Do not spoil what you have by desiring what you have not; remember that what you now have was once among the things you only hoped for." — Epicurus

"Don't grieve. Anything you lose comes around in another form." — Rumi, *Selected Poems*

"Every second you spend thinking about what somebody else has is taking away from time that you could create something for yourself." — Gary Vaynerchuk

"You have a unique gift to offer this world. Be true to yourself, be kind to yourself, read and learn about everything that interests you and keep away from people who bring you down. When you treat yourself kindly and respect the uniqueness of those around you, you will be giving this world an amazing gift... YOU!" — Steve Maraboli, *Unapologetically You*

"Do not have evil-doers for friends, do not have low people for friends: have virtuous people for friends, have for friends the best of men." — Gautama Buddha, *The Dhammapada*

"Gratitude unlocks the fullness of life. It turns what we have into enough, and more. It turns denial into acceptance, chaos to order, confusion to clarity. It can turn a meal into a feast, a house into a home, a stranger into a friend." — Melody Beattie, *The Language of Letting Go*

"If you have a book, you have a friend." — Frank Delaney

"I have inner peace; I have accomplished a great deal." — Neil Sedaka

"I felt once how simple and frugal a thing is happiness: a glass of wine, a roast chestnut, a wretched little brazier, the sound of the sea. Nothing else." — Nikos Kazantzakis, *Zorba the Greek*

"One way to open your eyes is to ask yourself, 'What if I had never seen this before? What if I knew I would never see it again?'" — Rachel Carson, *The Sense of Wonder*

"Do what you can, with what you have, where you are." — Theodore Roosevelt, *The Works of Theodore Roosevelt*

"The earlier you learn that you should focus on what you have, and not obsess about what you don't have, the happier you will be." — Amy Poehler

"Success is not getting what you want, it's enjoying what you have." — Glen Campbell

"You have to not let yourself believe you can't. Do what you can do within the framework of what you have, and don't look outside – look inside." — Melvin Van Peebles

"Happiness doesn't depend on how much you have to enjoy, but how much you enjoy what you have." — Tom Wilson

"Never forget the three powerful resources you always have available to you: love, prayer, and forgiveness." — H. Jackson Brown, Jr., *Life's Instructions for Wisdom, Success, and Happiness*

"Clean water and access to food are some of the simplest things that we can take for granted each and every day. In places like Africa, these can be some of the hardest resources to attain if you live in a rural area." — Marcus Samuelsson

"Wealth consists not in having great possessions, but in having few wants." — Epictetus, *The Philosophy of Epictetus*

"Your vision will become clear only when you can look into your own heart. Who looks outside, dreams; who looks inside, awakes." — Carl Jung, *Letters*

"Having a superpower has nothing to do with the ability to fly or jump, or superhuman strength. The truest superpowers are the ones we all possess: willpower, integrity, and most importantly, courage." — Jason Reynolds

"One who has no love in his heart will try to possess everything for himself. One who has love in his heart is ready to sacrifice everything, including his own body, for the benefit of others." — Thiruvalluvar

"There is nothing wrong with men possessing riches. The wrong comes when riches possess men. — Billy Graham

"Love is really the only thing we can possess, keep with us, and take with us." — Elisabeth Kübler-Ross

"Almost every man wastes part of his life attempting to display qualities which he does not possess." — Samuel Johnson, *The Rambler*

"I really believe that everyone has a talent, ability, or skill that he can mine to support himself and to succeed in life." — Dean Koontz

"Gratitude means to recognize the good in your life, be thankful for whatever you have, some people may not even have one of those things you consider precious to you (love, family, friends etc.). Each day give thanks for the gift of life. You are blessed." — Pablo Valle

"To be upset over what you don't have is to waste what you do have." — Ken Keyes, Jr.

"Be content with what you have; rejoice in the way things are. When you realize there is nothing lacking, the whole world belongs to you." — Lao Tzu, *Tao Te Ching*

"Never pass up an opportunity to speak a kind word of appreciation. There are six billion people on the planet, and 5.9 billion of them go to bed every night starving for one honest word of appreciation." — Matthew Kelly, *The Rhythm of Life*

"Become aware that you already possess all the inner wisdom, strength, and creativity needed to make your dreams come true. This is hard for most of us to realize because the source of this unlimited personal power is buried so deeply beneath the bills, the car pool, the deadlines, the business trip, and the dirty laundry that we have difficulty accessing it in our daily lives. When we can't access our inner resources, we come to the flawed conclusion that happiness and fulfillment come only from external events. That's because external events usually bring with them some sort of change.... We can learn to be the catalysts for our own change .... You already possess all you need to be genuinely happy." — Sarah Ban Breathnach, *Simple Abundance*

"I believe one of our souls' major purposes is to know, love, and express our authentic selves. To live the life and be the person we were created to be. However, our true selves only emerge when it's safe to do so. Self-condemnation, shame, and guilt send your true nature into hiding. It's only in the safety of gentle curiosity, encouragement, and self-love that your soul can bloom as it was created to do." — Sue Patton Thoele

"The eighteenth-century German philosopher Johann Herder taught that each person has an original and unique manner of being human. The task is to develop it. According to Nietzsche, a person is known by his or her 'style,' that is, by the unique pattern that gives unity and distinctiveness to a person's activities. Style articulates the uniqueness of the self. Rather than fitting one's life into the demands of external conformity, rather than living one's life as an imitation of the life of another, one should look to find the authentic self within. One should labor to develop one's own unique style in crafting one's soul. An individual who denies his or her own individuality articulates life with a voice other than that which is uniquely his or her own. A person who suppresses his or her own self is in danger of missing the point of his or her own existence, of surrendering what being human means." — Byron Sherwin, *Crafting the Soul*

"When I see someone smile, I know immediately that he or she is dwelling in awareness. This half-smile, how many artists have labored to bring it to the lips of countless statues and paintings? I am sure the same smile must have been on the faces of the sculptors and painters as they worked. Can you imagine an angry painter giving birth to such a smile? Mona Lisa's smile is light, just a hint of a smile. Yet even a smile like that is enough to relax all the muscles in our face, to banish all worries and fatigue. A tiny bud of a smile on our lips nourishes awareness and calms us miraculously. It returns us to the peace we thought we had lost." — Thich Nhat Hanh

"Just imagine becoming the way you used to be as a very young child, before you understood the meaning of any word, before opinions took over your mind. The real you is loving, joyful, and free. The real you is just like a flower, just like the wind, just like the ocean, just like the sun." — Don Miguel Ruiz

"Sometimes I was so busy being tuned in to outside ideas, expectations, and demands, I failed to hear the unique music in my soul. I forfeited my ability to listen creatively to my deepest self, to my own God within." — Sue Monk Kidd

"The easiest thing in the world to be is you. The most difficult thing to be is what other people want you to be. Don't let them put you in that position." — Leo Buscaglia, *Love*

"Remember to be grateful. Feeling blessed by what others give to you, recognizing their contributions, and spending time cultivating your relationships with family and friends is critical to finding happiness in life."— Sonia Sotomayor

"My mission in life is not merely to survive, but to thrive; and to do so with some passion, some compassion, some humor and some style." — Maya Angelou

"Nobody is a villain in their own story. We're all the heroes of our own stories." — George R. R. Martin

"One day, after a drawing exercise, one of my students said in amazement, "Every time I draw something I fall in love!" I wasn't surprised to hear this, because I know that when we wake up to the world around us in full form, with vivid colors, lines, and shapes, we become filled with awe and wonder. It is easy to fall in love with the things we've walked past so many times, because we realize that the world is offering itself to us like a lover longing for our embrace and recognition. Receiving the universe in all its diversity allows us a new self-appreciation, and coming to a level of self-acceptance and self-love prepares us to love the world in return. When this awareness lives at our core, celebration becomes a way of life."— Adriana Diaz

"The most beautiful experience we can have is the mysterious. It is the fundamental emotion that stands at the cradle of true art and true science." — Albert Einstein, *The World as I See It*

"You have to know what you stand for, not just what you stand against." — Laurie Halse Anderson, *Speak*

"Creativity, decisiveness, passion, honesty, sincerity, love. These are the ultimate human resources. And when you engage these resources, you can get any other resource on Earth." — Tony Robbins

"Let us be grateful to the people who make us happy; they are the charming gardeners who make our souls blossom." — Marcel Proust, *Pleasures and Days*

"This being human is a guest house. Every morning is a new arrival. A joy, a depression, a meanness, some momentary awareness comes as an unexpected visitor. Welcome and entertain them all! Treat each guest honorably. The dark thought, the shame, the malice, meet them at the door laughing, and invite them in. Be grateful for whoever comes, because each has been sent as a guide from beyond." — Rumi, *The Guest House*

"Reflect upon your present blessings — of which every man has many — not on your past misfortunes, of which all men have some." — Charles Dickens, *A Christmas Carol and Other Christmas Writings*

"I am grateful for what I am and have. My thanksgiving is perpetual. It is surprising how contented one can be with nothing definite — only a sense of existence. Well, anything for variety. I am ready to try this for the next ten thousand years, and exhaust it. How sweet to think of! My extremities well charred, and my intellectual part too, so that there is no danger of worm or rot for a long while. My breath is sweet to me. O how I laugh when I think of my vague indefinite riches. No run on my bank can drain it, for my wealth is not possession but enjoyment." — Henry David Thoreau, *Letters to Various Persons*

"And when you crush an apple with your teeth, say to it in your heart:
Your seeds shall live in my body,
And the buds of your tomorrow shall blossom in my heart,
And your fragrance shall be my breath,
And together we shall rejoice through all the seasons." — Kahlil Gibran, *The Prophet*

"I give myself a good cry if I need it, but then I concentrate on all good things still in my life." — Mitch Albom, *Tuesdays with Morrie*

"Ask not that events should happen as you will, but let your will be that events should happen as they do, and you shall have peace." — Epictetus, *The Discourses*

"Don't say you don't have enough time. You have exactly the same number of hours per day that were given to Helen Keller, Pasteur, Michelangelo, Mother Teresa, Leonardo da Vinci, Thomas Jefferson, and Albert Einstein." — H. Jackson Brown, Jr., *The Complete Life's Little Instruction Book*

"'Crises' can help us discover much about ourselves and enrich our lives. If 'disaster' enriches our lives with gifts that would otherwise have been taken for granted, is it really a disaster? Or is it a gift in disguise?" — Elisabeth Kübler-Ross

Focus on the Present,
Not on the Past and Future

"Do not dwell in the past, do not dream of the future, concentrate the mind on the present moment." — Gautama Buddha

---

"For me, looking back is akin to being on a tightrope and looking down. It doesn't help you in the present moment to deal with what you have to deal with in order to move forward." — The Edge

---

"To get over the past, you first have to accept that the past is over. No matter how many times you revisit it, analyze it, regret it, or sweat it...it's over. It can hurt you no more." — Mandy Hale, *The Single Woman*

"It's a terrible thing, I think, in life to wait until you're ready. I have this feeling now that actually no one is ever ready to do anything. There is almost no such thing as ready. There is only now. And you may as well do it now. Generally speaking, now is as good a time as any." — Hugh Laurie

---

"The power for creating a better future is contained in the present moment: You create a good future by creating a good present." — Eckhart Tolle

"Breathe. Let go. And remind yourself that this very moment is the only one you know you have for sure." — Oprah Winfrey

"How wonderful it is that nobody need wait a single moment before starting to improve the world." — Anne Frank, *Anne Frank's Tales from the Secret Annex*

"People are capable at any time in their lives, of doing what they dream of." — Paulo Coelho, *The Alchemist*

"Change your life today. Don't gamble on the future, act now, without delay." — Simone de Beauvoir

"We are living in a culture entirely hypnotized by the illusion of time, in which the so-called present moment is felt as nothing but an infinitesimal hairline between an all-powerfully causative past and an absorbingly important future. We have no present. Our consciousness is almost completely preoccupied with memory and expectation. We do not realize that there never was, is, nor will be any other experience than present experience. We are therefore out of touch with reality. We confuse the world as talked about, described, and measured with the world which actually is. We are sick with a fascination for the useful tools of names and numbers, of symbols, signs, conceptions and ideas." — Alan Watts

"You can't afford to think about what might have been. You just be aware of what is." — Noel Gallagher

"Nature does not hurry, yet everything is accomplished." — Lao Tzu, *Tao Te Ching*

"I'm not saying you shouldn't pursue dreams and goals. Just don't forsake the present for the unknowns of the future. A lot of happiness is bypassed, overlooked, postponed to a time years from now that may never come. Don't bide your time and miss out on this moment for a tomorrow with no guarantee." — Kim Holden, *Bright Side*

"Do not be anxious about tomorrow, for tomorrow will be anxious for itself. Let the day's own trouble be sufficient for the day." — Matthew 6:34, *The Bible*

"Finish each day and be done with it. You have done what you could. Some blunders and absurdities no doubt crept in; forget them as soon as you can. Tomorrow is a new day. You shall begin it serenely and with too high a spirit to be encumbered with your old nonsense." — Ralph Waldo Emerson

"Each morning when I open my eyes I say to myself: I, not events, have the power to make me happy or unhappy today. I can choose which it shall be. Yesterday is dead, tomorrow hasn't arrived yet. I have just one day, today, and I'm going to be happy in it." — Groucho Marx

"One of the key qualities a leader must possess is the ability to detach from the chaos, mayhem, and emotions in a situation and make good, clear decisions based on what is actually happening." — Jocko Willink

"Somebody should tell us, right at the start of our lives, that we are dying. Then we might live to the limit, every minute of every day. Do it! I say. Whatever you want to do, do it now! There are only so many tomorrows." — Michael Landon

"For a long time it seemed to me that real life was about to begin – real life. But there was always some obstacle in the way. Something had to be got through first, some unfinished business, time still to be served, or a debt to be paid. Then life would begin. At last it dawned on me that these obstacles were my life." — Alfred D'Souza

"You never know when a moment and a few sincere words can have an impact on a life." — Zig Ziglar

"You don't get to choose how you're going to die. Or when. But you can decide how you're going to live now." — Joan Baez, *Daybreak*

"Do not carry the burden of the past; do not live in the future. The only important thing is that one lives in the present authentically and fully. Whatever your current life is, be the most you can be by living in the moment." — Chan Chih

"You cannot afford to wait for perfect conditions. Goal setting is often a matter of balancing timing against available resources. Opportunities are easily lost while waiting for perfect conditions." — Gary Ryan Blair

"To become mindfully aware of our surroundings is to bring our thinking back to our present moment reality and to the possibility of some semblance of serenity in the face of circumstances outside our ability to control." — Jeff Kober

"Life gives you plenty of time to do whatever you want to do if you stay in the present moment." — Deepak Chopra

"The present moment, if you think about it, is the only time there is. No matter what time it is, it is always now." — Marianne Williamson

"There are certain ways in which I cultivate awareness, both through mindful yoga and taking care of my body and taking time to actually drop as deeply as possible into stillness, into whatever is unfolding in the present moment." — Jon Kabat-Zinn

"Meditation has taught me to be in the present moment and observe the present moment at the same time. Just breathe, follow your breath, and your intuition can take you from there." — Tara Stiles

"Our present moment is a mystery that we are part of. Here and now is where all the wonder of life lies hidden. And make no mistake about it, to strive to live completely in the present is to strive for what already is the case." — Wayne Dyer

"There are plenty of reasons to put our cell phones down now and then, not least the fact that incessantly checking them takes us out of the present moment and disrupts family dinners around the globe." — Amy Cuddy

"What is the biggest thing that stops people from living their lives in the present moment? Fear – and we must learn how to overcome fear." — Brian Weiss

"To be wronged is nothing unless you continue to remember it." — Confucius

"Children have a way of forcing you back into the present moment." — Lorna Luft, *Me and My Shadows*

"There is surely nothing other than the single purpose of the present moment. A man's whole life is a succession of moment after moment. If one fully understands the present moment, there will be nothing else to do, and nothing else to pursue. Live being true to the single purpose of the moment."— Yamamoto Tsunetomo, *Hagakure*

"I know that the purpose of life is to understand and be in the present moment with the people you love. It's just that simple." — Jane Seymour

"Learn to enjoy every minute of your life. Be happy now. Don't wait for something outside of yourself to make you happy in the future. Think how really precious is the time you have to spend, whether it's at work or with your family. Every minute should be enjoyed and savored." — Earl Nightingale

"Always do your best. What you plant now, you will harvest later." — Og Mandino

"Planning is bringing the future into the present so that you can do something about it now." — Alan Lakein

"Let us make our future now, and let us make our dreams tomorrow's reality." — Malala Yousafzai

"It's being here now that's important. There's no past and there's no future. Time is a very misleading thing. All there is ever, is the now. We can gain experience from the past, but we can't relive it; and we can hope for the future, but we don't know if there is one." — George Harrison

"I don't live in either my past or my future. I'm interested only in the present. If you can concentrate always on the present, you'll be a happy man. Life will be a party for you, a grand festival, because life is the moment we're living now." — Paulo Coelho, *The Alchemist*

"Hell is in the here and now. So is heaven. Quit worrying about hell or dreaming about heaven, as they are both present inside this very moment. Every time we fall in love, we ascend to heaven. Every time we hate, envy, or fight someone, we tumble straight into the fires of hell." — Elif Shafak, *The Forty Rules of Love*

"To the attentive eye, each moment of the year has its own beauty, and in the same fields, it beholds, every hour, a picture which was never seen before, and which shall never be seen again." — Ralph Waldo Emerson, *Nature and Selected Essays*

"There is no other day. All days are present now. This moment contains all moments." — C. S. Lewis, *The Great Divorce*

"For unless one is able to live fully in the present, the future is a hoax. There is no point whatever in making plans for a future which you will never be able to enjoy. When your plans mature, you will still be living for some other future beyond. You will never, never be able to sit back with full contentment and say, 'Now, I've arrived!' Your entire education has deprived you of this capacity because it was preparing you for the future, instead of showing you how to be alive now." — Alan Watts, *The Book on the Taboo Against Knowing Who You Are*

"Love isn't a state of perfect caring. It is an active noun like struggle. To love someone is to strive to accept that person exactly the way he or she is, right here and now." — Fred Rogers, *The World According to Mister Rogers*

"If we take care of the moments, the years will take care of themselves." — Maria Edgeworth

"No man ever steps in the same river twice, for it's not the same river and he's not the same man." — Heraclitus

"Remember then: there is only one time that is important – Now! It is the most important time because it is the only time when we have any power. The most necessary man is he with whom you are, for no man knows whether he will ever have dealings with anyone else: and the most important affair is, to do him good, because for that purpose alone was man sent into this life!" — Leo Tolstoy, *What Men Live by and Other Tales*

"If you feel anxiety or depression, you are not in the present. You are either anxiously projecting the future or depressed and stuck in the past. The only thing you have any control over is the present moment; simple breathing exercises can make us calm and present instantly." — Tobe Hanson, *The Four Seasons Way of Life*

"It stands to reason that anyone who learns to live well will die well. The skills are the same: being present in the moment, and humble, and brave, and keeping a sense of humor." — Victoria Moran, *Younger By the Day*

"Enjoy present pleasures in such a way as not to injure future ones." — Seneca, *Letters from a Stoic*

Focus on What You Need,
Not on What You Want

"Distinguish between real needs and artificial wants and control the latter." — Mahatma Gandhi

"A deep sense of love and belonging is an irreducible need of all people. We are biologically, cognitively, physically, and spiritually wired to love, to be loved, and to belong. When those needs are not met, we don't function as we were meant to. We break. We fall apart. We numb. We ache. We hurt others. We get sick." — Brené Brown, *The Gifts of Imperfection*

"Continuous learning is the minimum requirement for success in any field." — Brian Tracy

"If we have love, we have family, we have everything we need." — Ayesha Curry

"I may not have gone where I intended to go, but I think I have ended up where I needed to be." — Douglas Adams, *The Long Dark Tea-Time of the Soul*

"The most valuable of all education is the ability to make yourself do the thing you have to do, when it has to be done, whether you like it or not." — Aldous Huxley

"Nothing is particularly hard if you divide it into small jobs." — Henry Ford

"I went to the woods because I wished to live deliberately, to front only the essential facts of life, and see if I could not learn what it had to teach, and not, when I came to die, discover that I had not lived."— Henry David Thoreau, *Walden*

"When you read about the lives of other people, people of different circumstances or similar circumstances, you are part of their lives for that moment. You inhabit their lives, and you feel what they're feeling, and that is compassion. If we see that reading does allow us that, we see how absolutely essential reading is." — Amy Tan

"It's not the daily increase but daily decrease. Hack away at the unessential." — Bruce Lee

"Housing is absolutely essential to human flourishing. Without stable shelter, it all falls apart." — Matthew Desmond

"Self-esteem is as important to our well-being as legs are to a table. It is essential for physical and mental health and for happiness." — Louise Hart

"For me, it is essential to have the inner peace and serenity of prayer in order to listen to the silence of God, which speaks to us, in our personal life and the history of our times, of the power of love." — Adolfo Perez Esquivel

"Effective tidying involves only three essential actions. All you need to do is take the time to examine every item you own, decide whether or not you want to keep it, then choose where to put what you keep. Designate a place for each thing." — Marie Kondo

"Passion for what you do is essential to success in any profession. That passion naturally keeps you interested and aware of everything that is going on around you, anything affecting your craft." — Daniel Humm

"The best and most beautiful things in the world cannot be seen or even touched – they must be felt with the heart." — Helen Keller

"We must develop and maintain the capacity to forgive. He who is devoid of the power to forgive is devoid of the power to love. There is some good in the worst of us and some evil in the best of us. When we discover this, we are less prone to hate our enemies." — Martin Luther King, Jr.

"Most of the things we buy are wants. And we call them needs, but they're wants." — Dave Ramsey

"After nourishment, shelter and companionship, stories are the thing we need most in the world." — Philip Pullman

"A man travels the world over in search of what he needs and returns home to find it." — George A. Moore, *The Brook Kerith*

"Man needs so little… yet he begins wanting so much." — Louis L'Amour

"A friend is what the heart needs all the time." — Henry Van Dyke

"Everything happens when it needs to happen; everyone is always where they need to be. You will never miss out on what is meant for you, even if it has to come to you in a roundabout way." — Iyanla Vanzant

"The world needs less heat and more light. It needs less of the heat of anger, revenge, retaliation, and more of the light of ideas, faith, courage, aspiration, joy, love, and hope." — Wilferd Peterson

"A truly strong person does not need the approval of others any more than a lion needs the approval of sheep." — Vernon Howard

"They say a person needs just three things to be truly happy in this world: someone to love, something to do, and something to hope for." — Tom Bodett, *As Far as You Can Go Without a Passport*

"The world needs different kinds of minds to work together." — Temple Grandin

"The most basic of all human needs is the need to understand and be understood. The best way to understand people is to listen to them." — Ralph Nichols

"Wilderness is not a luxury but a necessity of the human spirit, and as vital to our lives as water and good bread." — Edward Abbey, *Desert Solitaire*

"You never truly need what you want. That is the main and thoroughgoing key to serenity." — Albert Ellis

"No need to hurry. No need to sparkle. No need to be anybody but oneself." — Virginia Woolf, *A Room of One's Own*

"Remember, if you ever need a helping hand, it's at the end of your arm, as you get older, remember you have another hand: The first is to help yourself, the second is to help others." — Audrey Hepburn

"I don't need a friend who changes when I change and who nods when I nod; my shadow does that much better." — Plutarch

"For millions of years, mankind lived just like the animals. Then something happened which unleashed the power of our imagination. We learned to talk and we learned to listen. Speech has allowed the communication of ideas, enabling human beings to work together to build the impossible. Mankind's greatest achievements have come about by talking, and its greatest failures by not talking. It doesn't have to be like this. Our greatest hopes could become reality in the future. With the technology at our disposal, the possibilities are unbounded. All we need to do is make sure we keep talking." — Stephen Hawking

"Maybe there aren't any such things as good friends or bad friends — maybe there are just friends, people who stand by you when you're hurt and who help you feel not so lonely. Maybe they're always worth being scared for, and hoping for, and living for. Maybe worth dying for too, if that's what has to be. No good friends. No bad friends. Only people you want, need to be with; people who build their houses in your heart." — Stephen King, *It*

"Feet, what do I need them for if I have wings to fly." — Frida Kahlo

"I don't owe people anything, and I don't have to talk to them any more than I feel I need to." — Ned Vizzini, *It's Kind of a Funny Story*

"Sometimes you need to take a break from everyone and spend time alone, to experience, appreciate, and love yourself." — Robert Tew

"For good ideas and true innovation, you need human interaction, conflict, argument, and debate." — Margaret Heffernan

"Reading is essential for those who wish to rise above the ordinary. We must not permit anything to stand between us and the books that could change our lives." — Jim Rohn

"I'm starting to think this world is just a place for us to learn that we need each other more than we want to admit." — Richelle E. Goodrich, *Smile Anyway*

"It's been proven by quite a few studies that plants are good for our psychological development. If you green an area, the rate of crime goes down. Torture victims begin to recover when they spend time outside in a garden with flowers. So we need them, in some deep psychological sense, which I don't suppose anybody really understands yet." — Jane Goodall

"The pain is necessary. Sometimes pain is the teacher we require, a hidden gift of healing and hope." — Janet Jackson

"Tolerance, inter-cultural dialogue and respect for diversity are more essential than ever in a world where peoples are becoming more and more closely interconnected." — Kofi Annan

"Disconnecting from our technology to reconnect with ourselves is absolutely essential for wisdom." — Arianna Huffington

"Spending time alone in your own company reinforces your self-worth and is often the number-one way to replenish your resilience reserves." — Sam Owen, *Resilient Me*

"The hardest thing to find in life is balance - especially the more success you have, the more you look to the other side of the gate. What do I need to stay grounded, in touch, in love, connected, emotionally balanced? Look within yourself." — Celine Dion

Focus on What You Can Give,
Not on What You Can Take

"You give but little when you give of your possessions. It is when you give of yourself that you truly give." — Kahlil Gibran, *The Prophet*

"I don't think you ever stop giving. I really don't. I think it's an ongoing process. And it's not just about being able to write a check. It's being able to touch somebody's life." — Oprah Winfrey

"Forgiveness. It's one of the greatest gifts you can give yourself, to forgive. Forgive everybody. You are relieved of carrying that burden of resentment. You really are lighter. You feel lighter. You just drop that." — Maya Angelou

"When you take a flower in your hand and really look at it, it's your world for the moment. I want to give that world to someone else. Most people in the city rush around so, they have no time to look at a flower. I want them to see it whether they want to or not." — Georgia O'Keeffe

"We make a living by what we get, but we make a life by what we give." — Winston Churchill

"My father gave me the greatest gift anyone could give another person, he believed in me." — Jim Valvano

"The greatest gift that you can give to others is the gift of unconditional love and acceptance." — Brian Tracy

"God gave us the gift of life; it is up to us to give ourselves the gift of living well." — Voltaire

"The worth of a human being lies in the ability to extend oneself, to go outside oneself, to exist in and for other people." — Milan Kundera, *Laughable Loves*

"You only have what you give. It's by spending yourself that you become rich." — Isabel Allende

"All things will be produced in superior quantity and quality, and with greater ease, when each man works at a single occupation, in accordance with his natural gifts, and at the right moment, without meddling with anything else." — Plato, *Republic*

"Each day provides its own gifts." — Marcus Aurelius

"We really have to understand the person we want to love. If our love is only a will to possess, it is not love. If we only think of ourselves, if we know only our own needs and ignore the needs of the other person, we cannot love." — Thich Nhat Hanh, *Peace Is Every Step*

"If I were given the opportunity to present a gift to the next generation, it would be the ability for each individual to learn to laugh at himself." — Charles M. Schulz

"Imagine what a harmonious world could be if every single person, both young and old, shared a little of what he is good at." — Quincy Jones

"I hope that my achievements in life shall be these – that I will have fought for what was right and fair, that I will have risked for that which mattered, and that I will have given help to those who were in need, that I will have left the earth a better place for what I've done and who I've been." — C. Hoppe

"My greatest accomplishments shall never be known, perhaps even to me. Having made someone smile and see the world a bit brighter, having given someone hope for the future, having helped someone see potential inside him or herself that he or she never might have seen otherwise, having helped someone to see just how beautiful he or she really is – these to me are the achievements that most can help this world to be a brighter, more loving place." — Tom Walsh

"The task is to recognize that you are uniquely special, have something to give, some talent no one else shares in quite the same way. This gift needs to blossom so we can appreciate and enjoy the benefits of it and acknowledge you for it. You owe this to yourself and to all of us to honor your gifts, for only when you share your unique joy with the world does the entire world benefit. Every advance mankind has known has come because of someone's effort. Don't let shyness rob you and the world of the power and the passion that lies within you. No one can be all that you will be except you yourself. Follow your passion." — Joel Garfinkle

"Someone I loved once gave me a box full of darkness. It took me years to understand that this too, was a gift." — Mary Oliver, *Thirst*

"Maybe some people just aren't meant to be in our lives forever. Maybe some people are just passing through. It's like some people just come through our lives to bring us something: a gift, a blessing, a lesson we need to learn. And that's why they're here. You'll have that gift forever." — Danielle Steel, *The Gift*

"You have a grand gift for silence, Watson. It makes you quite invaluable as a companion." — Sherlock Holmes (Sir Arthur Conan Doyle), *The Complete Sherlock Holmes*

"Ruin is a gift. Ruin is the road to transformation." — Elizabeth Gilbert, *Eat, Pray, Love*

"The greatest gifts you can give your children are the roots of responsibility and the wings of independence." — Denis Waitley

"Those who are happiest are those who do the most for others." — Booker T. Washington, *Up from Slavery*

"The law of giving is very simple: if you want joy, give joy. If love is what you seek, offer love. If you crave material affluence, help others become prosperous." — Deepak Chopra, *The Seven Spiritual Laws of Success*

"Don't give to get. Give to inspire others to give." — Simon Sinek

"Love grows by giving. The love we give away is the only love we keep. The only way to retain love is to give it away." — Elbert Hubbard

"Be helpful. When you see a person without a smile. Give them yours." — Zig Ziglar

"The measure of your life will not be in what you accumulate, but in what you give away." — Wayne Dyer, *Staying on the Path*

"Give yourself credit. It takes courage to start over and reach for a better life. Many people never even try. Their fear, insecurity, and lack of belief in their personal power hold them hostage, sometimes forever. Acknowledge, thank and appreciate yourself for being brave enough to try. At every step along the way, give yourself your love, support and recognition."— Cynthia Occelli

"There is nothing more beautiful than someone who goes out of their way to make life beautiful for others." — Mandy Hale, *The Single Woman*

"Life's most persistent and urgent question is, 'What are you doing for others?'" — Martin Luther King, Jr., *Strength to Love*

"If you're in the luckiest one per cent of humanity, you owe it to the rest of humanity to think about the other 99 percent." — Warren Buffett

"It's not enough to have lived. We should be determined to live for something. May I suggest that it be creating joy for others, sharing what we have for the betterment of personkind, bringing hope to the lost and love to the lonely." — Leo Buscaglia, *Love*

"Strong people don't put others down... They lift them up." — Michael P. Watson

"If you're not making someone else's life better, then you're wasting your time. Your life will become better by making other lives better." — Will Smith

"I cannot do all the good that the world needs. But the world needs all the good that I can do." — Jana Stanfield

"One of the most important things you can do on this earth is to let people know they are not alone." — Shannon L. Alder

"Sometimes those who give the most are the ones with the least to spare." — Mike McIntyre, *The Kindness of Strangers*

"Never underestimate the difference YOU can make in the lives of others. Step forward, reach out and help. This week reach to someone that might need a lift." — Pablo Valle

"Helping others is the secret sauce to a happy life." — Todd Stocker, *Refined*

"When you reach out to those in need, do not be surprised if the essential meaning of something occurs." — Stephen Richards

"Life is not easy for any of us. But what of that? We must have perseverance and, above all, confidence in ourselves. We must believe we are gifted for something and that this thing must be attained." — Marie Curie

"The simple gift of giving becomes an elaborate rich aftertaste of a natural blissful feeling, lingering endlessly in my lifetime." — Wes Adamson

"To do more for the world than the world does for you – that is success." — Henry Ford

"The best way to find yourself is to lose yourself in the service of others." — Mahatma Gandhi

"If you wait until you can do everything for everybody, instead of doing something for somebody, you'll end up not doing nothing for nobody." — Malcom Bane

"A man has made at least a start on discovering the meaning of human life when he plants shade trees under which he knows full well he will never sit." — D. Elton Trueblood, *The Life We Prize*

"The level of our success is limited only by our imagination and no act of kindness, however small, is ever wasted." — Aesop

"What we have done for ourselves alone dies with us, what we have done for others and the world remains and is immortal." — Albert Pike

"Good actions give strength to ourselves and inspire good actions in others." — Plato

"What you leave behind is not what is engraved in stone monuments, but what is woven into the lives of others." — Pericles

"The single most beautiful gift you can give to others is your positive attitude." — Jacqueline Camacho-Ruiz

3 Bonus Quotes to Ponder

"With an open mind, seek and listen to all the highest ideals. Consider the most enlightened thoughts. Then choose your path, person by person, each for oneself." — Zoroaster

"Every day you must unlearn the ways that hold you back. You must rid yourself of negativity, so you can learn to fly." — Leon Brown

"We are not given a good life or a bad life, we are given a life and it's up to us to make it good or bad." — Ward Foley

An Excerpt from *7 Thoughts to Live Your Life By*

On the following pages is a free sample of the companion to this book, which is a book that I strongly recommend reading to help you put into action the quotes you have read here. The title is *7 Thoughts to Live Your Life By: A Guide to the Happy, Peaceful, & Meaningful Life.*

Here is what readers have said about the book:

"If everyone would read this book – and implement the Seven Thoughts as described here – life would be a lot less stressful, kinder, and a more humane, peaceful and positive experience." — Steven Howard, Author, Leadership Development Facilitator

"Our thoughts really are like rivers, that may wander, meander or trickle or rush. Sometimes our thoughts flow nicely, and all is in order and is nurtured. This book is different to other self-help books about managing your own thoughts, because this book presents the information in a multi-dimensional perspective. Others give the principles flatly or one dimensionally, meaning they are really like orders or commands, but with no unifying substance. This is the best general self-help book that I have read." — Celine Lai, Book blogger

An Introduction to the 7 Thoughts to Live Your Life By

"We are shaped by our thoughts; we become what we think. When the mind is pure, joy follows like a shadow that never leaves." – Buddha

What are the Ultimate Goals of this Book?

The goal of *7 Thoughts to Live Your Life By* is to transcend the goals of self-improvement books. What does this mean? Whether your goal is happiness, peace, finding your purpose, spiritual healing, productivity, success, wisdom, sociability, clear thinking, or something else that involves improving yourself, I believe you will find what you need here. Ultimately, this book will provide you with a unifying framework to help you maximize your potential.

Let's consider what separates this book from the many others which you may have read.

You may have heard that in warfare, or in strategy games, that there are *tactics* and there are *strategies*. Tactics are generally seen as concrete actions you can take to solve a specific problem. Self-development books generally focus on this. A focus on tactics can be helpful because often, you have a specific problem, and you need it solved. For example, if you want help with making new friends, then you may find a book that deals with this specific issue.

In contrast, strategies are built around *not* solving one particular problem, but in planning and putting yourself in the best position to deal with *any* problems that may arise. Although this book does include tactics and concrete tips, it includes them in a way that is ultimately strategic, and that will help you put yourself in the best position to deal with the primary obstacles of your life. *7 Thoughts to Live Your Life By* may not show you how to solve your immediate problem, but it will be your toolkit for understanding how to make the best use of your mind, and to use it to its full powers to solve your everyday problems. This approach should ultimately be more effective.

A further goal of this book will be to help you attain clarity and focus of the mind. We live in a world overloaded with information – which can be found via the internet, books, news, television, radio, gurus, and so forth. With so much information available, and so much new information being made available daily, it can be difficult to create a calm and focused mind. Our minds tend to go in all directions and accomplish little in the end.

The fundamental idea of *7 Thoughts to Live Your Life By* is that if we could calm the mind and focus on what truly mattered, then we would be much happier, more at peace, and ultimately able to live a life full of meaning.

As a final point, I would like to mention that I have occasionally received emails from people who will explain to me what their life problem is. I have noticed that typically their misery comes from *not* having applied the *7 Thoughts* in their lives. In many cases this is simply because they are not aware of their existence. I have observed this quite often, in fact, and I have found it frustrating to know that their issues could be resolved in a straightforward manner if only they had the same insights that I have had – with this book, now of course it is possible for you to gain those insights.

Before delving into the Thoughts, allow me to share some of my background with you in the following section.

A Destructive Force Within…

Now, let's begin with my life, and what drove me to write this book in the first place.

I spent, or perhaps *wasted*, years of my life. I spent that time in a negative haze, with a dark cloud hanging over me. I had problems with being sociable, so I assumed that people didn't enjoy being with me and that they did not like me. It was a great struggle for me to be around people, because I felt that they were thinking negatively about me. I didn't sense it at the time, but my issue was more with my internal negativity, rather than any true negativity on their part. Sometimes, people even asked me, "Why are you so negative? What is wrong?" But I never had a good answer. My belief was that reality actually was negative and terrible, and that I simply had to deal with it. I didn't understand that I was being consumed by my own negativity at the time – and that my way of seeing life didn't represent reality.

However maladaptive my negative way of thinking was, by my early twenties I was getting used to it. I thought that the negativity was a part of who I was – that it was in my personality. My life had evolved into a bad habit of seeing, thinking, and doing in a negative way. Of course, I was not happy about this – but at the same time, I didn't see any other options. I didn't know any other way to be. I felt entrapped, but I couldn't grasp any way out of the reality that I had created for myself.

This way of being lasted for many years, and then came the toughest period of my life. I had applied to a graduate school program in industrial-organizational psychology. I had a deep doubt within me, realizing that I would be tested beyond what I could even imagine. A part of me knew that I was not ready for this program, but I applied anyway. On paper, I was an excellent student, but my communication skills were quite poor, and I was worried about this. Nonetheless, I was accepted into the program.

In the first week, I realized that this would be the biggest challenge of my life. However, the work itself wasn't overly difficult, intellectually. Rather, there was so much work that needed to be done, that there appeared to be no end in sight to it. For example, there was a heavy load of course work, multiple research projects, learning to use statistical programs, management of undergraduate researchers, many administrative tasks, and a variety of meetings per week on research topics, all while I was adjusting to living in a new state.

My biggest battle at the time, however, was not the work itself, nor in adjusting to the new location. It was in learning to deal with my own overwhelming negativity. The force of it was becoming greater and greater, as it gained in power under the increasing pressures and stresses of my life.

Even in the first few weeks of the program, I did not think that I could deal with all of the work. I felt like I was being suffocated under all of it. I had so much to do and learn that it was overwhelming, beyond anything I could have expected. I had begun to lose confidence that I would be able to do all the tasks required of me. Failure was often on my mind – I sensed that it was inevitable.

After several months in the program, I felt defeated. I was keeping up with the work demands, but my mind was telling me that I was going to fail, over and over, and I was not happy. Work occupied my mind all day long, and when it was time to sleep, I could not stop thinking about it. Generally, I would only sleep a few hours per night. I was also losing weight, and I was already thin when the program had begun. A big sign that my mind was malfunctioning was that I was forgetting very simple things. I would forget meeting times and sometimes I could not recall what someone had said to me only moments earlier.

At my worst, my mind was occupied with incessant negative thoughts about myself – which is clearly counterproductive. I may have been sitting in a meeting, and my mind would wander into negative thoughts. I couldn't focus on anything else but this negativity. Eventually, I did not want to be in the program any longer. But I continued with it nonetheless.

After a few more months it was winter break. I should have been happy, but instead I found myself bedridden. I spent most of the days in bed, not because of a physical ailment – but because of a mental one. The negativity inside of me was on permanent full throttle now. Imagine getting into your car, putting it in neutral, and then putting your foot down on the gas all the way. The engine is revving so hard that it sounds like it could break, but the car isn't going anywhere. This is what my mind and my life had become. My mind was working in overdrive to the point of self-destruction, but I was not making progress. The fact that I was in bed, unable to do much of anything, only reinforced the negative thoughts I had had – that I was truly not going to be able to continue with the program.

As a simple example of just how bad things were, I found it difficult to do a basic task such as brushing my teeth – even this took all of my energy to accomplish. Sometimes I would feel good that I had managed to do this on my own, and then I would go back to bed and wonder:

If this is what I have stooped to, how will I ever continue with this graduate program? How will I ever finish my degree? If brushing my teeth is difficult, how can I learn advanced statistics and manage undergraduate students, or even show up to meetings or classes?

I thought seriously about whether it was even worth it to continue. But I somehow realized that my mind wasn't working properly, and I didn't feel qualified to make such a big decision in that state of mind, so I didn't quit.

In reality, the program was becoming less of a concern – my life itself was now my biggest problem. If I continued to deteriorate at this rate, I would have much bigger problems than just finishing a graduate program.

After this lowest of lows, spending most of my days in bed, I decided to finally get some help and I went to my doctor. I was given some tests, and he explained that I had major depressive disorder *and* dysthymia. He prescribed some antidepressants and he told me to start seeing a clinical psychologist to receive some counseling. He said that in my deeply depressed state, it was critical that I take the medication *and* attend the counseling. Either one alone would not be sufficient.

After a few weeks of following the treatment, I was well enough to function again. I could do basic tasks, but it was still a struggle to operate at the higher level that the graduate program required. After a few months, I was doing fine. I was no longer overwhelmed by a self-created negativity, and I was able to do all of my work without much trouble.

The true healing would take many years, however. The medication and therapy helped to reset my mind and body, but I was not truly healed. I still needed to learn to control my mind to prevent this from ever happening again. After a couple of years on the treatment plan, with the aid of my doctor and therapist, I stopped taking the medication and I stopped going to counseling. I felt the need to do this so that I could control my own destiny fully. I wanted to be sure that *I* was the master of my own mind, and that I didn't need to rely on either medication or counseling. I intuitively knew that I didn't need it – my biggest problem was a self-created negativity, and therefore I could learn to control it.

In the months after stopping treatment I didn't feel worse, but I still didn't feel happy, or like I was on a path that I looked forward to pursuing. I wasn't overwhelmed with negativity, but I didn't view this alone as a true success. It's as much of a success as you would say being absent of pain is a success. The achievement of not being profoundly empty or sad just wasn't enough. There needed to be more to life than just this. *I wanted something more.*

As an important note, if you want to stop taking a medication or stop a counseling program, be sure to discuss this with your medical and counseling professionals first. There can be great risks with stopping either one suddenly, depending on your situation.

The Path to True Healing

Realizing that my life was not yet on its proper course, I reflected on why some things had gone so wrongly. In fact, I often reflected on this. Clearly, my focus on everything negative had not helped. It seemed as if my natural focus on the negative had spiraled out of control, and I was unable to tame it after it had gained a certain degree of momentum. However, I felt like there was something more that I was missing, so I continued to reflect, day after day. Ultimately, this was not bringing me any new insights, and so I realized that I needed to change my approach.

Then I began meditating. I believed that doing this could help me to control my own negativity, which it did. But ultimately, what surprised me was that I sometimes had deep insights into myself or about the world that arose through these meditations. My system was that I would enter a peaceful meditative state, and in a deep focused state I was often able to perceive lucidly. Then, I would ask myself a question on how to live a better life, and how to overcome my problems.

One day while meditating, these Thoughts all flooded into me:

1. Focus on what you can control, *not* on what you cannot control
2. Focus on the positive, *not* the negative
3. Focus on what you can do, *not* on what you cannot do
4. Focus on what you have, *not* on what you do not have
5. Focus on the present, *not* on the past and future
6. Focus on what you need, *not* on what you want
7. Focus on what you can give, *not* on what you can take

I believe my mind had synthesized *all* of the mistakes I had made in my life. It had examined the numerous mistakes and missteps that had led me into a life of growing negativity, to the point that this negative force had become greater than the force of my own true self. In meditation, my mind realized that it was itself, *my own mind*, which had become the enemy. Thus, through an intuitive and synthetic process, I came up with these Thoughts to help prevent the mind from becoming a destructive force, and to allow it to flourish and become a constructive force – a force for good rather than a force for bad.

Essentially, in my personal life, I had been focusing on the opposite of these Thoughts, and so intuitively, my mind must have realized that this had been the source of my problems. I needed to have a dynamic shift, a shift of the mind into the opposite of what it had once been. It would be a transformative process. My challenge would be to flip my focus completely – and to turn everything around. I wrote down the *Thoughts*, and I began using them as a guide post. I started living my life by the 7 Thoughts, and from then on, my life was never the same. True change didn't happen overnight. It took years, in fact, but every time I repeated these thoughts to myself, as if they were a mantra, I felt at peace sensing that I was moving along the right path. Things would be alright in the end.

Why are These Thoughts So Important?

I find that when I stray from these Thoughts, and I allow myself to go with the crowds and fall into negative patterns and worry about what is outside of my control and dwell on the past, that things start to fall apart. Depression and anxiety are not far off. Often, I diverge from the Thoughts just a little bit, then a little bit more, and then I find that I am quickly becoming lost at sea – surrounded by a turbulent storm. Luckily, when I have noticed this, I have been able to navigate myself back to safety. This has happened several times, and I am only more convinced that to live a good life, it is critical to follow these Thoughts *every day*. Following these Thoughts forces me to be fully conscious about my thoughts, so that I can learn to attract the good thoughts and to let the bad ones flow out of me. When I stop giving fuel and energy to those bad thoughts, they tend to go away in time.

I am aware that sometimes authors get excited about an idea or a system that they have only used briefly, and they want to write a book about it. I would like to be clear that the background of this book is nothing like that. I originally had these Thoughts 7 years before the publication of this book. In that time, I have reflected on these Thoughts deeply, and incorporated them into my life. At times, I would briefly forget about them, but every time I did I realized that I had made a big mistake, and I would incorporate them into my life once again.

Our true task, which this book shall help with, is to *turn the destructive mind into a constructive mind*. This isn't to say that your whole mind is destructive, but perhaps parts of it are. Then, wouldn't it be best to flip those parts of your mind around and make them work for you in a positive way?

Of course it would.

Before continuing, I need to mention that since coming up with the Thoughts in meditation, I have realized that they are everywhere. They appear in religious texts, philosophical works, fables and parables, psychological studies, and in everyday maxims or sayings that people say. The fact that they appear over and over in a wide range of important texts, and in the words of a wide range of gurus throughout a span of millennia, shows just how important these Thoughts are. As you can see, I did not discover these Thoughts. They were always there, and I simply rediscovered them for myself. They are common and yet hidden away, because most of us don't follow them since we are bombarded by thousands of thoughts and pieces of information daily. It is time for us to clear the clutter, and to prioritize the Thoughts in our lives.

The Top Three Ingredients to Living the Good Life

A key aim of the *7 Thoughts to Live Your Life By* is to help you to live a good life. Here, I will discuss the top three ingredients that you will need for this: Purpose, Success, and Happiness.

Purpose

What is your purpose? Do you know? What is your WHY? Why do you do anything? Only you can figure this out, but if you have not, I would urge you to view this as the central issue of your life until you do figure it out. Understand that your purpose is not limited to a field of study. For instance, your purpose is not to be a doctor, it is to save lives. Your purpose is not to be an architect, it is to build the most beautiful or the safest building that ever existed. Your purpose is not to be an artist, it is to make the world come to life with beautiful art that makes people wonder about what is possible. The book *Mastery* by Robert Greene helped me not only to realize my purpose, but to have the courage to pursue it whole-heartedly.

Create your own *life purpose statement*. Think about what you truly want to get out of life, and how you can get to that point. What do you want to provide for others? What is the most personally fulfilling thing you could do? If you feel like you need more experience or knowledge to figure out your purpose, acquire it. For example, you may contact an expert and interview him or ask how you can be of help. An expert is more likely to help you learn if you commit to helping him, rather than if you focus on what he will give to you. Through helping, of course, you will learn greatly.

Make your life purpose statement short and direct. I would recommend that it be either one sentence or two short sentences if possible. When you have crafted it, put it in a prominent place where you cannot forget about it. Also, it does not have to be static. In time, you may choose to modify it or even start over from scratch.

Success

"Your level of success will seldom exceed your level of personal development." – Jim Rohn

Ultimately, we all need to define what success means for us. However, I believe most people have a limited view of what success is, and I would urge you to consider my definition below.

Success = Energy + Morals + Purpose

A foundation of your success will be your energy levels. We tend to take this for granted, but you need to be feeling good and have a strong vitality to be in the best position to succeed. Even for those of us who appear to be in great general health, we should always dedicate some time to keeping ourselves healthy and energetic. As we know, this involves a combination of eating healthy, exercise, sleeping well, and stress management. In general, I would also recommend that you do things that make you feel more energized and avoid those that do not. For instance, if driving aggravates you and drains your energy, it may be better to find someone who can drive you, or to ride a bike.

Next, success is about sticking to moral principles, because if you don't, then any "success" you achieve is tainted by misdeeds you may have committed to meet that achievement. At its core, morality is about treating others as you would like to be treated, and about being truthful with yourself and others. There is not a specific moral code that you must follow, rather, it will be important for you to do what you know to be right on your path to success.

Also, success ultimately happens when you are living out your life's purpose. You may be in a life situation that makes it difficult to live out your purpose – but I believe it will be worth pursuing with all of your heart and might. If you don't, you will always wonder what could have been. You must understand that true success comes when you find a way to live your purpose, even if that purpose is not defined by your job. The two do not always overlap. A key way to live out your purpose is to make the most of any special skills you may have, or your gift (See 7th Thought). But ultimately, only you can decide your true purpose.

Happiness

To me, happiness is being free to express yourself, it is being as healthy as you can be, alert, energetic, and able to feel at a full range of emotion and not restricted to always being rational or emotional. Happiness is to be in sync with your morals, to be in the pursuit of meeting your purpose, and to be your true self, not a false created self that you feel other people want you to be. Of course, happiness is to have love in your life, which could come from family or a spouse, or with other people that you develop close connections with. To be happy, it is not required that you have a favorable life. It is possible for a dying person to be happy, or even someone who is in prison to be happy. Happiness is doing your best, but ultimately accepting yourself, people, and situations as they are. It means being able to control your mind (See 1st Thought) so that you can be in a positive state (See 2nd Thought), regardless of the situation or environment.

The ancient Greeks believed that happiness was something that could not be fully judged about a person until their death. Someone may be happy in one moment or another, but to know if they were truly happy, we must look at their full life.

Your Thoughts Will Rule Your Life – Choose them Carefully

"Happiness is when what you think, what you say, and what you do are in harmony." – Mahatma Gandhi

I present the quote above as a reminder. Many of us have thoughts that are completely incongruent with the person that we truly want to be. But rather than change those original thoughts, we learn to justify our actions. Instead, we should go back to square one and examine the thoughts that we choose to have, because from there, they have great influence over what we say and do.

Many of us think of thoughts as *just thoughts*. They are harmless, perhaps even meaningless, you may think. I will show you that this is far from being true.

In reality, the sum of your thoughts leads to the sum of your actions, which leads to the sum of who you are. Many people understand that they are the sum of their choices and of their actions. What they don't always fully understand is that they are also the sum of their thoughts. Their thoughts lead to their actions.

Allow me to elaborate.

Your thoughts will become manifest in your expressions (e.g., such as facial expressions) – and your expressions are contagious. If you have a sad expression, it is much more likely you will make others feel this too. If you smile happily, you may have this effect on those around you as well.

Your thoughts will become what you say – and what you say is mimicked by others. Just as your expressions are contagious, so is what you say. Have you ever noticed that you may hear a new phrase, and soon after this you start to hear it all of the time? A catchy expression is mimicked by many and it quickly becomes the go-to catch phrase of the public.

Your thoughts will become your actions – which model behaviors for others. Actions are also contagious. If you spend a great deal of time with someone, you may find that you start to do some of the same things.

Even if this person has strange or unique habits, you may find yourself mimicking this person, perhaps unconsciously.

Your actions will become reactions in others – and those reactions will mimic the original action. For instance, aggression tends to create the reaction of aggression. Love tends to create the reaction of love. Fear in one person tends to spread that fear to those who are nearby. It does not always work this way, but if you perform an action, you are much more likely to create that same reaction in someone else.

In summary, your thoughts will become contagious in others – in the form of expressions, words, actions, and reactions that will pass on as if an echo. When you speak in a small room, you will hear your own echo. Similarly, everything you think, say, and do forms a sort of echo reaction in the world around you. You will not be able to perceive that echo, because unlike an echo of sound that reflects back at you almost immediately, the echo of your thoughts and actions passes through the world slowly, but it ripples through the universe for eternity. In fact, much of what we are doing today is the result of the echoes of prior generations – what they thought, what they said, and what they did.

Have you ever noticed that there is truth to the saying that we become our parents? Of course, we get to choose our own actions and we are not limited to being who our parents are, but in times of stress or when we are tired or don't have time to think, our default actions are likely to fall back to what we have seen our parents do. You may find yourself repeating phrases that your parents would say, in the same situations that they would have said them. This is an example of the echoes through time, of people's thoughts, words, and actions. Perhaps your children will feel the same, and use the same phrases at those same moments, and perhaps their children too. Our thoughts, words and actions transcend ourselves, spreading as if a virus – this can be a good thing if they are positive and bad if they are negative.

Understand that what you think ends up creating the entire world around you. Of course, this effect is hard to see because of the slow echoing, but also because we are all playing a role in the thoughts, words, and actions that get passed on, and which ultimately become contagious. Since we are one person of many billions in this world, we feel like what we think, say, and do does not matter. But it does. Your thoughts can propel you forward or drag you down, and they can do the same for countless other people – having a big impact on the people who you surround yourself with.

The implications here can run deep. The world becomes influenced by what you think, and it reacts to you based on what you think of the world. What you think is reflected back onto you. If you are in love with the world, you receive a loving energy back. If you are angry at the world, you receive an angry energy back. Thus, you must mind your thoughts. Be careful what you think, because what you focus on and what you think will take up a bigger space in your life.

Remember this: Mind your mind. Mind your thinking. What we think has a way of manifesting itself into reality.

The 7 Thoughts that Help Us to Live the Good Life

The following are the 7 Thoughts which will be the focus of this book:

1. Focus on what you can control, *not* on what you cannot control
2. Focus on the positive, *not* the negative
3. Focus on what you can do, *not* on what you cannot do
4. Focus on what you have, *not* on what you do not have
5. Focus on the present, *not* on the past and future
6. Focus on what you need, *not* on what you want
7. Focus on what you can give, *not* on what you can take

While I came upon these thoughts during a meditative session, I have thought about them deeply and I would like to explain the logic of these Thoughts, and why they are ordered in this way.

By focusing on **what you can control**, you immediately prevent yourself from wasting your time, life, and energy on matters that are out of your influence and control. With this focus, you will realize that the #1 thing that you can control is your mind, and your mind performs much better when you **focus on the positive** instead of on the negative. However, if there is a problem in front of you, perhaps one that you have negative feelings about, then you must **focus on what you can do** to resolve this problem. Your focus will be on what is within your power. Just remember that what you can do is limited by what you have, or your resources. Thus, you must **focus on what you have**, because this is all that you can work with to resolve your problems. Logically, if you focus on what you have, then you need to **focus on the present moment** in your life, because this is all that you truly have. The past is done, and the future is uncertain. The present is where you influence the world around you and where you have control. In the present moment, you must keep perspective and prioritize what truly matters in your life – thus, **focus on what you need** above what you want. What you do not need, you may give away, to **give back to the world** which has given much to you.

Inspirational Figures

I always find it helpful to keep some inspirational figures in mind, to remember that we are capable of much more than we think we are. Here are just a few brief stories of people who have triumphed even when the odds were against them. I hope they inspire you as much as they have inspired me.

Malala Yousafzai

Malala is a young woman who stood up for the rights of girls like herself to pursue education, even when she was still a child living in Pakistan, a place where this was not a freely given right. What did she get for saying that all girls should have the right to education? Sadly, she was attacked, *receiving a bullet to the head.* Suddenly, Malala was fighting for her life. This attack proved the great dangers that any girl in Pakistan may face just for speaking her mind. Luckily, she did survive and recover from this horrible attack. Despite the incident, Malala never wavered in her message. Ultimately, she went on to win the Nobel Peace Prize in 2014, where she was commended for her "struggle against the suppression of children and young people and for the right of all children to education." Malala along with her Malala Fund – a nonprofit organization, has helped rebuild schools and is active in helping girls to have the right and the path to pursue 12 years of "free, safe, quality education."

William Kamkwamba

William was a young boy who grew up in extreme poverty in Malawi, Africa. His family was very poor and at one point he was unable to afford $80 that was required for him to attend school. Incredibly, this boy living in immense poverty was able to build a windmill to bring electric power to his village with a bare minimum of resources. Some materials that he used to do this were blue gum trees, bicycle parts, and other materials he had gathered from a local scrapyard. Importantly, he had often visited the village library and discovered books with pictures of windmills in them, which ultimately helped him to build his own. In 2014, he graduated from Dartmouth College and according to his *About* page on www.williamkamkwamba.com, "He is now working with WiderNet to develop an appropriate technology curriculum that will allow people to bridge the gap between 'knowing' and 'doing'."

Cruz Robledo

Cruz was a young man with a 7th grade education growing up in Mexico – making him the most educated person from his village at the time, in the early 1960s. His dream was to go to the US to pursue greater opportunities. In the small village where he was raised, education beyond around the 3rd grade level was considered a luxury that generally could not be afforded. However, Cruz showed a promising aptitude in school, and his father supported him financially so that he could reach the 7th grade. Unfortunately, the pressures on his father with raising a large family made it infeasible for him to continue funding Cruz's education beyond this point.

At 17 years old, Cruz decided to go to the US to pursue greater opportunities. He learned English and went to night school, and then he applied to Purdue University. They offered him admission, and he was immensely grateful for this opportunity. Being a student there was the greatest challenge of his life, as he realized that his educational background left him far behind the other students. By this point he was working full time, taking a full load of courses, and he had a family to support as well. Ultimately, despite the high level of challenge, he did graduate with his B. S. in agriculture. After working in his industry for a decade in the US, he started his own business in Mexico, where he provided and continues to provide research services for leading universities, companies, and institutions around the world. This man is my father, as you may have noticed that we have the same last name.

In all of these stories, we have individuals who were far, far behind everyone else. They had *fewer opportunities*, not more, and yet they managed to lead successful and fulfilling lives. Ultimately, they surpassed the majority of people who would have had many more advantages. I find it important to always keep these types of stories in mind. Whenever you doubt yourself and your situation, understand that many people have thrived even when having come from practically nothing.

Now that you know what is possible when you put your mind to it, I believe that you are in the right frame of mind to begin learning about the 7 Thoughts to Live Your Life By.

If you are interested in continuing to read *7 Thoughts to Live Your Life By*, you can learn more here:

https://mentalmax.net/7TB2R

Thank You

Thank you for taking the time to read *365 Quotes to Live Your Life By*. I hope that you found the information useful. Just remember that a key part of the learning process is putting what you read into practice.

Before you go, I want to invite you to pick up your free copy of *Step Up Your Learning: Free Tools to Learn Almost Anything*. All you have to do is type this link into your browser:

http://mentalmax.net/EN

Also, if you have any questions, comments, or feedback about this book, you can send me a message and I'll get back to you as soon as possible. Please put the title of the book you are commenting on in the subject line. My email address is:

ic.robledo@mentalmax.net

Did You Learn Something New?

If you found value in this book, please review it on Amazon so I can stay focused on writing more great books. Even a short one or two sentences would be helpful.

To go directly to the review page, you may type this into your web browser:

https://mentalmax.net/365QRev

An Invitation to the "Master Your Mind" Community (on Facebook)

I founded a community where we can share advice or tips on our journey to mastering the mind. Whether you want to think more positively, be a better learner, improve your creativity, get focused, or work on other such goals, this will be a place to find helpful information and a supportive network. I hope you join us and commit to taking your mind to a higher level.

To go directly to the page to join the community, you may type this into your web browser:

https://mentalmax.net/FB

More Books by I. C. Robledo

7 Thoughts to Live Your Life By – #1 Recommended Read

The Intellectual Toolkit of Geniuses

Master Your Focus

The Smart Habit Guide

No One Ever Taught Me How to Learn

55 Smart Apps to Level Up Your Brain

Ready, Set, Change

Smart Life Book Bundle (Books 1-6)

The Secret Principles of Genius

Idea Hacks

Practical Memory

7 Thoughts to Live Your Life By

Made in the USA
Columbia, SC
11 December 2023

28282147R00065